Ethical Internet Marketing

Jason Fladlien
&
Thom Lancaster

Dedicated to Internet Marketers everywhere, with thanks.

Ethical Internet Marketing

Table of Contents

About The Authors

Jason Fladlien is a former hip hop artist and house painter, who now makes a monthly 6 Figure income.

To find out more about Jason, visit JasonFladlienTraining.com.

Thom Lancaster is a UK based Internet Marketer. He has a particular interest in product creation.

To find out more about Thom, visit ThomLancaster.com.

Foreward

Does ethics have a place in Internet Marketing and in the wider business world?

Most people would say yes, without hesitation, but how many times have you struggled with personal ethics?

Have you had to give a refund to a customer who claims to have not received a product but you know has downloaded it? Would that be breaking your ethical code to refuse a refund under any circumstances?

Do you believe it's ever acceptable to be rude to a customer, or even 'fire' a customer? What if they're making unreasonable request – or unsuitable demands on your time?

The whole area of ethics is a minefield.

In **Ethical Internet Marketing** Jason Fladlien contends that ethics don't really have a place in business, and he supports his views with real world examples from his own business dealings.

However, Jason does have his own hierarchy of values, which he lives within.

This hierarchy, which largely breaks down into four rules, makes perfect sense. It

Jason FladlienTraining.com

provides a clear blueprint to use within your marketing career.

Even if you don't agree with all of Jason's rules, you should use these as a base, and then take these forward to develop your own hierarchy of values.

Thom Lancaster
ThomLancaster.com

Jason FladlienTraining.com

Chapter 1 - Introduction

Welcome to **Ethical Internet Marketing**. I'm Jason Fladlien.

In this book, I'm going to discuss with you what place do "ethics" have in business and in particular Internet Marketing.

I contest that ethics in business is overrated.

A lot of you have been pre-programmed with the wrong kind of philosophical attitude to have towards approaching your business, and I see it all the time. People try to guilt you into getting what they want out of you. So they're going to use all kinds of ethical concerns that are actually not in your best interest. You've got to have a bulletproof self-image to handle these. You got to come with your own ethical code for doing business.

There's a hierarchy of values that I take into account when I make my business decisions to coincide with ethics, and I'm going to share this with you; and like I said, this is so important because this will dictate a lot of your business decisions and also safe proof you from having that guilt that a lot of people are going to try to lay on you because it's complete crap.

I'm going to break this hierarchy of values down into four simple rules which I live by in Internet Marketing.

Let's get right to it.

Jason FladlienTraining.com

Chapter 2 – You're Not Here To Make Friends

Understand this. If you're in business you are in the "get money" business not the "make friends" business. The sole objective means make a profit without going to jail, without breaking any laws. That's basically your number one rule. You're in the make money business if you're in business. You are not in the make friends business. You can do that on your own time. You can do that during the weekend. You can do that with all the money you give that gives you the freedom to then take those final years of your life off you can be everybody's friend.

Now does it help to be nice? Yeah, it absolutely does. You can probably make more money being nice, but being nice on its own is not going to make you money, and in fact, it is not required to have a successful business.

Understanding is making more money -- and I'll give you the criteria here in a second. But being nice is not the #1 criterion for making money in the internet or anywhere -- in any business.

Jason FladlienTraining.com

Chapter 3 – You're Not Here To Make Good Products

Get this. Creating good products is not the #1 criterion for making money. Does it help? It absolutely does help, but again it is not required.

Here's the only thing that is required for you to make money on the internet. You have to find a way to get more in monetary return than you give in intangible value and tangible assets and resources. This is the only thing that's required. Everything else is secondary.

In this case I have to find a way, let's say, I knew a really good strategy for becoming an instant expert at something in as quickly as possible time. And it only took me an hour to share that with you. But I can clone a system and create a system through a couple hours of work for four hours of my time. But I give so much intangible value, meaning the value can't be measured in dollars necessarily, to the user so they feel like they're getting a good deal so I'm giving them a lot, and I'm getting a lot back in return.

But the four hours it takes me to create and create the passive system for that product, and I make $10,000 -- that is smart because that puts the value of my time at about $2,500, which is pretty good for me. I'm happy if I can do that. So in that case it's a smart business move. I don't have to be nice about it. I can be a complete asshole about it. I say, "This is how you are going do this, this is this, whatever." The product itself it might not be my best performance. It might be an average product. It might be below average. Maybe I don't do an adequate job of explaining it, but because the potential is there, and I can market it properly and help convey that to you that I can make money.

Jason FladlienTraining.com

Chapter 4 – Return More Then You Give

This is the #1 rule.

The first thing is creating a system for whatever what you offer you're going to get more in return. You are going get back more than what you put into it, and that doesn't mean you have to rip somebody off. There's a way, especially because you're selling intangibles here that you can give them something for where they feel they got more for their money, and you got more than what you put the time into. So everybody can win.

You just got to figure out a system to where you're happy with getting in return more than what you give. So that's the #1 rule, and you got to do that without breaking any laws basically without stealing, cheating, or breaking any laws. That is the overriding factor for making decisions.

Will it make me money that I am satisfied with making? Will it make me money that I am satisfied with making? Now will it make a bunch of other people happy and make them applaud me and say I am a nice person? Not. Will it make a bunch of people give me these great testimonials about how great the product was? Blah, blah, blah. No. The #1 factor is will it make me money.

Jason FladlienTraining.com

Chapter 5 – Making The Money You Want Ethically

If you've watched my business you'll see how I've applied rule #1.

I over-deliver, absolutely. I'm a nice guy, absolutely. But that is not my primary objective.

In business I figured out a way to get those while I go out to my primary objective, which is making the money I want in the timeframe I want. Because the next question you have to ask yourself is how long will it take me to make the money? Because there are three levels here.

There's short-term money, there's medium-term money, and there's long-term money. So some things you're going do aren't going to have immediate value that you can measure that'll have money in the long term. And there's some stuff that you need money right away so those are what you're going to focus on.

Ideally you have stuff that you're working on today, tomorrow, the next day, and forever, as long as you are working in your business that are going to make you money in the short term; some things you're doing that are going make you money in the long term; and some stuff that are going make you intermediate return on money in the medium-term.

Here's my own personal philosophy for making money with rule No. 1, Rule No. 1 is you have to find a way that's going make you more money than what you put into it, and then the second thing is find the way that's going make you as much money as possible for the time and resources you invested. That is rule No. 1

and you do all that without lying, cheating, stealing, or going to jail.

Here's my own personal philosophy. Make some of that time that you spend in your business devoted to making money ASAP, some of it with the medium making money in a month or two months or six months -- some of that in a long-term plan.

And here's my own personal philosophy...80 percent short-term tactics will eventually pretty much create enough of everything else, to take care of everything else. We are in a time when time moves so fast. And as the marketplace changes once every three months, it's insane, it's hard to plan past what will I do this week that will make me money next week?

The second thing you gotta do is, okay, what can I do this week that will help me to make money next week? Well guess what? You're going to have to have long-term strategies, too. What I have found is typically you can reinvent your business. So say you do a bunch of short-term stuff. You are going to have all these assets left over. So you are going to have seven products you created in the last six months.

Guess what? You are going to have all these customers from those seven products. What you can then do is use those customers, and then put them together with all the products and resources you have and create higher value still in the short term. So that's what I find.

The medium-term strategy is automatically taken care of in the short-term strategy. And the long-term plan is simply conduct your business day-to-day so you can remember it in the long term, but don't do it at the sake of sacrificing too many up front profits.

I like money and I like a lot of it and I like to have it as quickly as possible. So I'm focused mostly on my business and what I can do this week that is going to make me money next week. Now, however, I do set aside long-term strategy time each week.

That's where the other 20 percent of my business goes.

If I work 80 hours a week, 60 hours will be spent on the short term and 20 hours will be spent on the long term. The long term is stuff like building your brand so people can remember you. And the long term stuff is like I'm going to create assets that are going to slowly make me money at first, but over the long period of time should bring people in. I'm talking about stuff like articles and videos.

Some of the other stuff as I'm writing books that in the future I am going to use to help me get public speaking engagements. So I have the big overall view of where I want to be, but I'm mostly focused on the short term. What can I do this week that is going to make me money next week.

The medium takes care of itself when you bundle all together all the short-term tactics to create a bigger package, and the long-term strategy is those little tiny things that you're working on, off hours mostly. This is the extra stuff you do every week that's not going to make you money right away that you have time to fit in that's going to eventually raise your net worth.

So that's rule #1. That is the first thing I consider whenever I make a business decision or what I should do in my business. Rule #1 is always what can I do to give me the most amount of money in the least amount of time. Not being nice. Not creating the best products. Nothing but that. What can I do? As long as it's legal and doesn't go against anything that's going to make me feel gross and scummy. That's what I do.

Jason FladlienTraining.com

Chapter 6 — The Rule Of Over-Delivery

The rule #2 is how can I over-deliver? Once I think how I can make the most money in the least amount of time I say, "Okay, within that timeframe, within that plan, how can I best over-deliver?"

And I'm not doing this to win nice guy points. But I'm doing this because it is a very sound business move. And why? It increases the lifetime customer value. The lifetime customer value means, how much will the average customer spend with you over your life or over the life of that customer?

Let's say the average customer is with you for three years and during that three-year period they spend $1,126. Well what happens if you find a way to really give them even more than they expect on every purchase and that makes them more comfortable trying new stuff out with you? Well you can increase their purchase to $2,000 over that three-year period of time.

So I don't do it because I'm a nice guy. I don't do it because people tell me you have to over-deliver. I don't do it because they say, "Well, you're making so much money you should give more back." Blah, blah, blah. Trying to guilt you into giving me more because I'm really selfish. None of that crap.

I'm not doing it to win any nice guy points. I'm doing it because it's a sound business move; because in the end, again, it will make me as much money as possible with the least amount of effort. That's what I'm into.

Jason FladlienTraining.com

Chapter 7 – The "Champion Theory"

Rule #3 here is a very big rule. It's how can I make my champions happy. Let me give you the "champion theory."

The champion theory is -- and this is an 80-20 rule axiom. Twenty percent of your customers are going to give you 80 percent of your profits. So really don't give a shit about the rest of your customers unless you can move them up from a one-time purchaser to a repeat purchaser to an advocate who loves you to a champion who'll pretty much buy anything that you want and will join that illustrious 20 percent of people who'll give you 80 percent of their profits.

If you have to make a decision, and you're going to annoy one of four people, let's just say this, four people and you have to make a decision, and that decision is going to annoy three people but is going to make one person happy. Who do you make happy?

You make your champion happy even if you have to annoy all three other people. In fact, even if you had to make all the other three people happy and annoy off your champion, you're screwing yourself. Because those three people combined have less value than that one person who is a good customer of yours.

You want to build a business that suits your champions. So really in order to do that, you are going to have to do things that 80 percent of your customer base is not set for that. It can be helpful for them, but if it comes down to the brass tactics you have to give your time to a champion or to a client. You are going to have to say, "Sorry client. You are not a champion," and you are going to have to make a choice and that is going to step on somebody's toes.

Here is my philosophy again. I do not care if I annoy 80 percent of my customers if that means satisfying 20 percent of my champions, my best customers. Because I can always get a new customer on the front end, but somebody who's built themselves up to champion status in my business is extremely hard to replace.

And really it gives you freedom and this is what's fine. Money is attracted to freedom. You'll find this out. So when you start running your business by your rules and basically only cater to a small segment of your customers, then you are going to attract a lot more people into doing business with you, because you are different than everybody else. Everybody else is so afraid to offend people, and personally I'm only afraid to offend one people, and that's the people that give me 80 percent of my profits, the 20 percent of people. I try to satisfy them as much as possible.

Jason FladlienTraining.com

Chapter 8 – Dealing With Guilt

Here's an issue that comes up all the time regarding rule #3.

Guilt.

I will not be guilted into giving my time away for free.I had somebody e-mail me and say, "Boy Jason, you should give me free coaching. I'll totally be worthwhile. I have the vinegar running through my blood to really put to use what you say." And I honestly replied to him, I said, "No. I am not going to do that. The only way I am going to be able to give you value is if you pay me for it." And they try to e-mail me back, "Well, I'm sorry that all you care about is money."

And I'm like, when I do my business, that's pretty much what I do care about -- is money. When I'm not doing my business and I'm hanging out with my family, then I don't really have a concern with money. In fact, I take my money, and I spend it very freely on them. I love doing that. But when it comes time to make my money, I am not a charity. I am not Red Cross. I am not any of those things. I am in the business to make money, and if I have to sacrifice time I can spend with the people who are paying me thousands of dollars for my advice to give it to you for free, because you're promising me something that I have no faith in believing that you are going to deliver on, which is following my information I'm ripping everybody else off to satisfy you. So I would feel guiltier not charging you. So if I am going to charge you, I am going to take you seriously. I want to know that you are somebody who takes me seriously, and we're all going to win.

That's my ethical concern for people who want to try to say that I'm selfish, or I'm only in it for the money or whatever. No. I am only in it for the money when it comes time to do business. Outside of business,

Jason FladlienTraining.com

if you don't want to do business and want to hang out with me, you'll find I'm a very pleasant person. I'm fun to be with. But when it comes time to make money, I have stuff I have to do in my business; and one of them is not running a charity giving a bunch of stuff away for free. I will only give it away for free if it will make me money the next day or a week later or two weeks later

But I have no obligation -- this is another thing that you should not feel guilty about. I have no obligation to somebody's financial situation or the results. If they come to me and they say, "Jason, will you please just let me in this coaching program for free, because my back's against the wall, and I'm poor, and my house is going to foreclose next month if I don't save this money that I'm going to pay you."

I'm not going to give them a free pass. I'm going to say, "You know what? If I did this for you, this is not going to force you to man up and get the result that you want, and so I'm sorry, but I'm going to have to give this to somebody else who is a little more responsible, unless you think this is the course for you then you'll find a way to get that money if you absolutely think this is the course for you. I have no obligation for your financial situation. You've put yourself in this situation. However, I know if you follow my advice and you're a reasonable person, you will probably be able to get out of that financial situation. But, you have to take yourself seriously first. Otherwise I'm not going to be able to take you seriously."

And the other thing is that I am not financially obligated. I'm not obligated to your results meaning my job ends when I deliver when I say I'm going to deliver and what you paid me to deliver. If you simply take that and do nothing with it, then that's your fault, not my fault. That's your problem." I am not supposed to be the guy that's going call you up every day and say, "Hey, did you do that? Did you do that? Come on I want to give you results." I'm not going to say, "Well, I feel bad that you didn't do anything. Here's half of your money back." I've had people who have paid me $700 to take my courses and absolutely didn't even log in and access the information. I'm not going to give them a refund. I delivered on what I said I was going to deliver, and actually these people never asked me for one, which is cool. I'm not going to do it out of the kindness of my heart.

I'm not talking about refund policy. Any time anybody asks me for a refund I give that to them, and I do that again, not because I'm a good person, but because I want my business to be profitable and I know I don't want to have to hassle with the FTC or somebody breaking down my door saying that I didn't do something or ripped off somebody. So I give refunds if people ask for them, but I don't do it out of the kindness of my heart because you simply didn't try what I told you to try. I don't feel guilty if you paid me for something I told you what to do and then you didn't do it, because my obligation ends with doing what I've been paid to do, which is to give you the information that will put you in the situation to get the results.

You have to have that same ironclad attitude where you have no obligation for somebody else's financial situation or the results. Your obligation ends when you say you're going to do what you say you are going to do and then you do it. So if you tell somebody that you're going to give them results or their money back, than that's a different story. But your obligation ends when you deliver what you say you are going to deliver.

Jason FladlienTraining.com

Chapter 9 — Making Business Pleasurable

The final rule is very simple and I'm going to spell it out to you.

Rule #4 is how can I make business a pleasant experience? This fits in very well with rules #1 to #3.

Jason FladlienTraining.com

Let's assume I can find a way to make a profit — that's rule #1, how much profit can I make in as little time as possible? Then rule #2 is; okay, now I have that timeframe, and I have that strategy. What can I do to make sure I deliver as much as possible within that time? Okay, great. Rule #3 is how can I make sure what I'm delivering in that time is going to satisfy those 20 percent in my crowd of people that purchased from me that resulted in 80 percent of the profits; and then rule #4 is how can I make doing business with me a pleasant experience?

As you've read this book you probably thought Jason's kind of a negative guy. I'd like to say I'm an accurate guy. Because this is accurate because people all over

66

the world are going to try to guilt you into doing stuff for them for free because it's in their best interest. People all over the world are going to try to impose their ethics onto you. These ethics are wrong when it comes to business. There's a time and a place. It's situational ethics. A lot of these ethics are situational.

Would you steal? Are you bad for stealing? Well it depends. If you're stealing a bomb from somebody who's going to kill a thousand people, and you're stealing it to disarm it and make sure they don't kill anybody, then stealing is good. In fact, you are unethical if you have the ability to do so and you don't. But if you're stealing something just because it's sitting on a dresser drawer and you don't even need it and you're stealing it from somebody who is now going to starve to death, then stealing is wrong.

Well the same thing is true. It's nice to be a charitable person in certain situations. It's stupid to be a charitable person in other situations. It's nice to be a nice person in certain situations but stupid in other situations.

I'm just giving you the accurate point here. But when you do business with me, after I figure out how I can make the most amount of money in the least amount of time, over-deliver as much as possible, and make my 20 percenters happy that give me 80 percent of my profits, then it's like how can I make business with me as pleasant experience as possible.

So this means giving them their goods as quickly as possible; answering customer support in as friendly manner as possible. It doesn't mean that you have to be a slave to somebody else because that is not one of the things. That's way down on the list of being really there, being on point all the time.

Once you figured out how to do these three things than the afterthought is if I have enough time, how can I make this as pleasant an experience as possible? But if you have to sacrifice pleasantness at the sake of making profits, and at the sake of making your champions happy, sacrifice pleasantness because these are the three things that are most important than that.

But with that said, over time, you get better and quicker at making money so then you can make your doing business with you even more pleasant, which is a more long-term strategy. So this is good stuff, but again it's pragmatic reasons why you want to do this, because it will help you make more money, which is rule #1.

Chapter 10 – Contributing Outside Business

There you have it. I've shared with you rules #1 to #4 about how I do business as an Internet Marketer.

Now, notice what's not on the list.

How can I create more jobs for the economy? I'll tell you what, the best thing you can do for the economy is be rich. Not create more jobs. So when you are rich you are going to spend more money.

Okay, what's not on the list is how can I make everybody happy? That's impossible. Even Mother Teresa had enemies. Ghandi had people that hated him, and somebody eventually killed him. Martin Luther King -- somebody killed him. You can't make everybody happy so just make a lot of money instead.

How can I contribute to society? You should contribute to society. Yeah, I agree, but the best thing you can contribute to society is the best value you can make for the money to get the most money in the least amount of time.

Because typically you have to give something that a lot of other people need so that's how you contribute to society by making a lot of money.

How can I win humanitarian of the year? Very simple. Figure out a way to make a bunch of money really quickly so you can retire at a very young age, and spend the rest of your life doing all the humanitarian things so you don't have to do business. You can just do humanitarian stuff. There you go.

Jason FladlienTraining.com

Chapter 11 - Conclusion

Thanks for reading **Ethical Internet Marketing**. I've broken down how I see business into four simple rules and explained my reasoning.

This all shows you the place I see that ethics have in business and in marketing.

I hope this has been beneficial for you so that you're not going to carry around all this baggage that is detrimental to making money and actually get on with it.

75

Jason FladlienTraining.com

That means actually following this stance and start making money, with or without my code of ethics.

Jason Fladlien
JasonFladlienTraining.com